For Every Learner™

grade K

Sounds & Letters

3 Differentiated Activities for Every Skill

- Rhyming
- Beginning sounds
- Ending sounds
- Syllables
- Uppercase and lowercase letters
- Initial consonants
- Final consonants
- Word families
- Short vowels

Editorial Team: Becky S. Andrews, Diane Badden, Kimberley Bruck, Karen A. Brudnak, Kitty Campbell, Pam Crane, Chris Curry, Lynette Dickerson, Lynn Drolet, Sarah Foreman, Theresa Lewis Goode, Tazmen Hansen, Marsha Heim, Lori Z. Henry, Angela Kamstra-Jacobson, Debra Liverman, Dorothy C. McKinney, Thad H. McLaurin, Brenda Miner, Sharon Murphy, Jennifer Nunn, Tina Petersen, Gerri Primak, Mark Rainey, Greg D. Rieves, Kelly Robertson, Hope Rodgers, Eliseo De Jesus Santos II, Rebecca Saunders, Donna K. Teal, Joshua Thomas

www.themailbox.com

ISBN10 #1-56234-862-0 • ISBN13 #978-156234-862-5

Manufactured in the United States
10 9 8 7 6 5 4 3 2 1

Table of Contents

What's Inside

3 practice opportunities for every featured skill!

Extra Support ▲

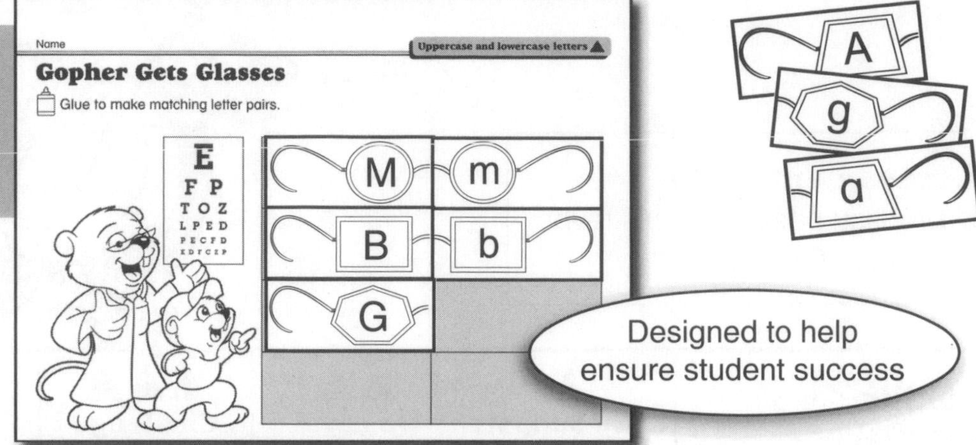

On Level ▲▲

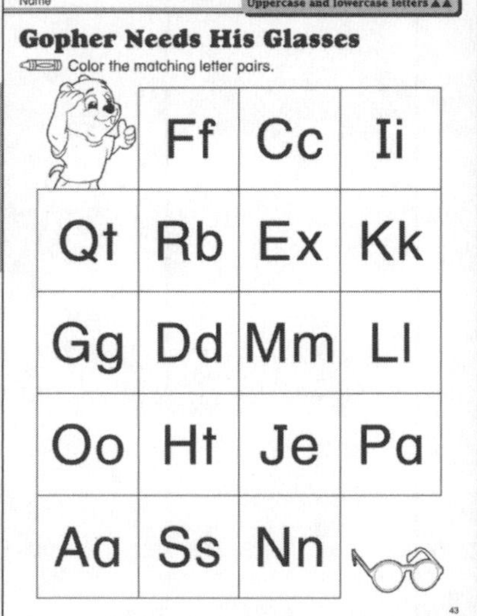
Name

Uppercase and lowercase letters ▲▲

Gopher Needs His Glasses

Color the matching letter pairs.

	Ff	Cc	Ii
Qt	Rb	Ex	Kk
Gg	Dd	Mm	Ll
Oo	Ht	Je	Pa
Aa	Ss	Nn	

43

Choose the right practice for each learner!

Challenge ▲▲▲

Name

Uppercase and lowercase letters ▲▲▲

Gopher's Reading Glasses

Write to make matching letter pairs.

b ___ E ___

A ___ K ___ I ___ j ___

G ___ V ___ c ___ D ___

m ___ T ___ L ___ o ___

S ___ n ___ Q ___ u ___

f ___ R ___ P ___ W ___

H ___ y ___ X ___ z ___

44

Same skill with an extra challenge

Name

Skills Checklist

Assessment Code
M = More practice needed at this level
S = Successful at this level

Skills	▲ Extra Support	▲▲ On Level	▲▲▲ Challenge	Notes
Rhyming pictures: set 1				
Rhyming pictures: set 2				
Beginning sounds: /b/, /m/				
Beginning sounds: /r/, /s/, /t/				
Beginning sounds: /g/, /n/, /p/				
Beginning sounds: /d/, /k/, /l/				
Ending sounds: /l/, /n/, /t/				
Beginning/ending sounds: /g/				
Word parts				
Uppercase/lowercase letters				
Initial consonants: *b, c, m*				
Initial consonants: *g, h, t*				
Initial consonants: *n, r, s*				
Initial/final consonants: *p*				
Word families: *-an, -at*				
Word families: *-ig, -in*				
Word families: *-op, -ot*				
Short vowels: *a, i*				
Short vowels: *e, o, u*				

Note to the teacher: To track the skill progress of individual students, personalize copies of the page. Each time a student completes a practice page, use the provided code to note an assessment of his work.

Name

Taking a Trip

Glue to match the rhyming pictures.

Note to the teacher: Have each child cut out a copy of a card set from page 6 before she begins the activity.

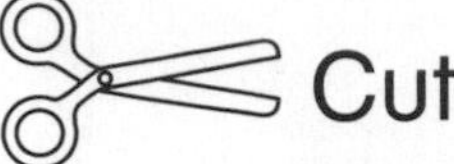

Cut.

Sort by the rhyming pictures.

Rhyming pictures ▲

Cut.

Sort by the rhyming pictures.

Note to the teacher: Use with "Taking a Trip" on page 5.

Name

On Our Way!

Color the rhyming pictures in each box.

Name

Toot! Toot!

Do all the pictures in each row rhyme?

Circle **Yes** or **No.**

	Yes / No
	Yes No
	Yes No
	Yes No
	Yes No
	Yes No
3	Yes No

If the answer is **No,** cross out the picture that does not rhyme.

Name

Pretty Presents

Glue to match the rhyming pictures.

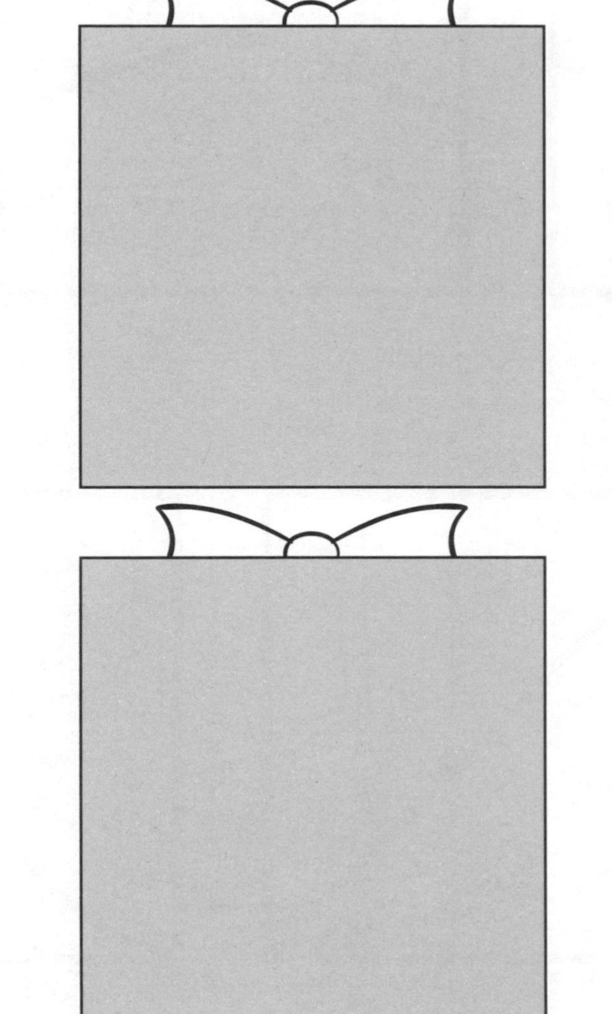

Note to the teacher: Have each child cut out a copy of the puzzles from page 10 before she begins the activity.

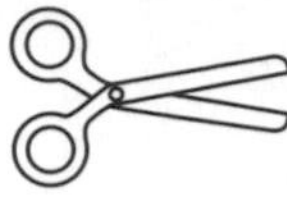

Cut the puzzles apart.
Mix the pieces.
Match the rhyming pairs.

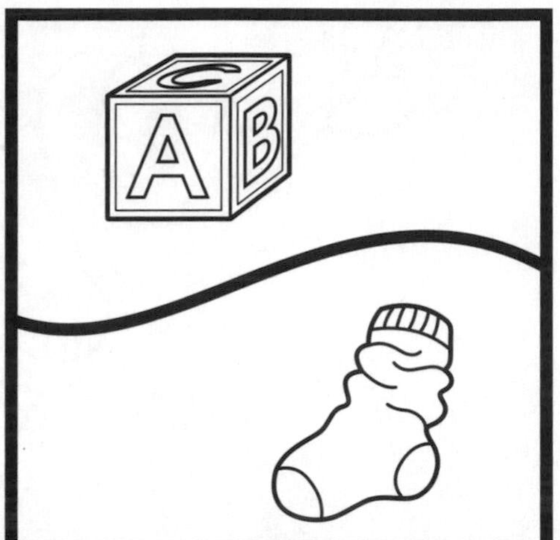

 Note to the teacher: Use with "Pretty Presents" on page 9.

Name

Tasty Cake!

Color the pictures that rhyme with key.

Name

Party Time!

Color by the code.

Color Code

rhymes with  — yellow
rhymes with  — orange
rhymes with  — red

WELCOME

Name

Hide-and-Seek

Glue to match the beginning sounds.

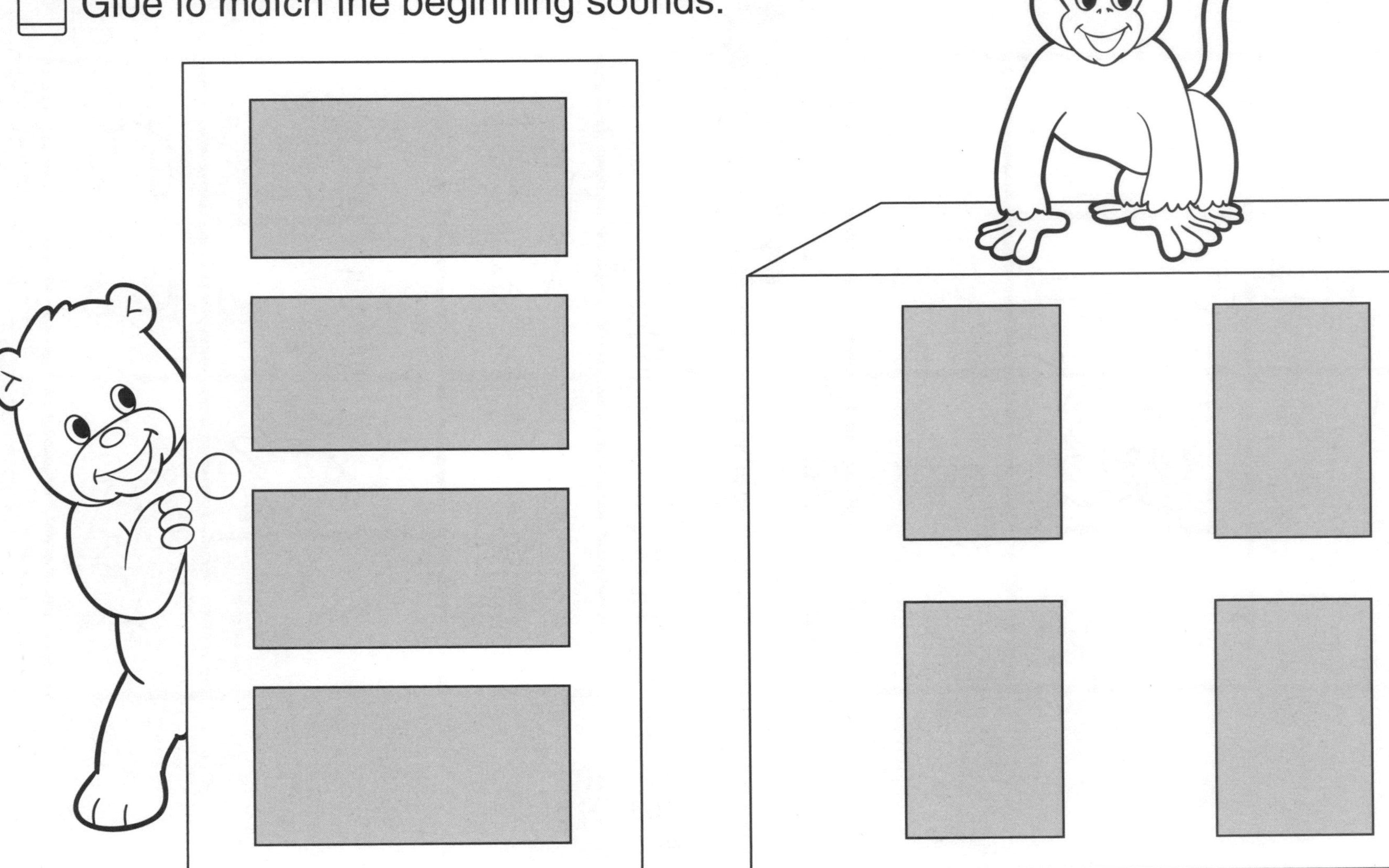

Note to the teacher: Have each child cut out a copy of a card set from page 14 before she begins the activity.

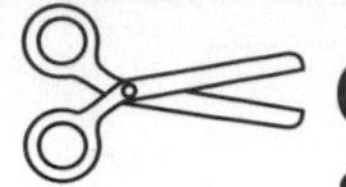

Cut.
Sort by the beginning sounds.

Beginning sounds: /b/, /m/ ▲

Cut.
Sort by the beginning sounds.

 Note to the teacher: Use with "Hide-and-Seek" on page 13.

Name

Having a Ball!

Color by the code.

Color Code

starts like (bear) —yellow   starts like (monkey) —red

Name

Best Friends

Name the pictures in each row.
Cross out the picture that begins with a different sound.

Name

Cozy Campsite

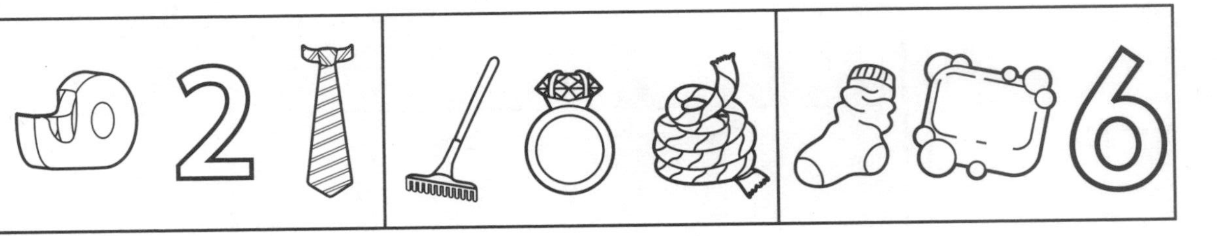

Color the 3 pictures in each row with the matching beginning sound.

Name

Packing for Camping

Glue to match the beginning sounds.

10

Note to the teacher: Have each child cut out a copy of a card set from page 19 before he begins the activity.

Cut.

Beginning sounds: /r/, /s/, /t/ ▲▲

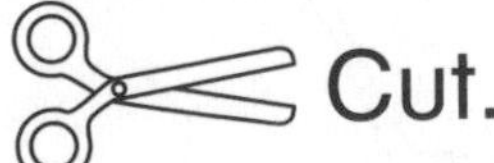
Cut.

Note to the teacher: Use with "Packing for Camping" on page 18.

Name

Looking at the Stars

Color by the code.

Cross out the pictures that have a different beginning sound.

2

Color Code

starts like — yellow

starts like — red

starts like — green

Name

Beginning sounds: /g/, /n/, /p/

Friendly Football

Cut.

Glue to match the beginning sounds.

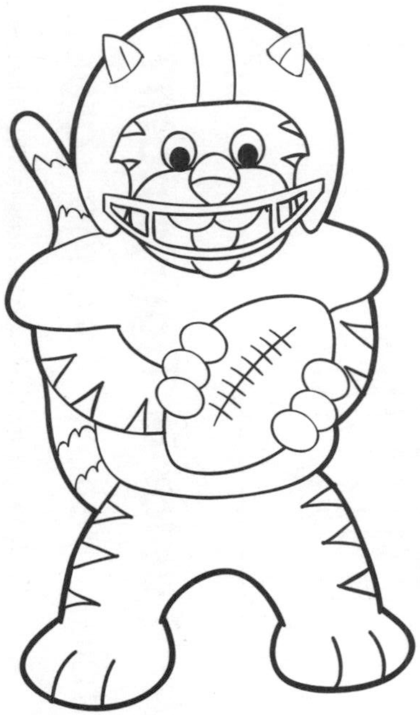

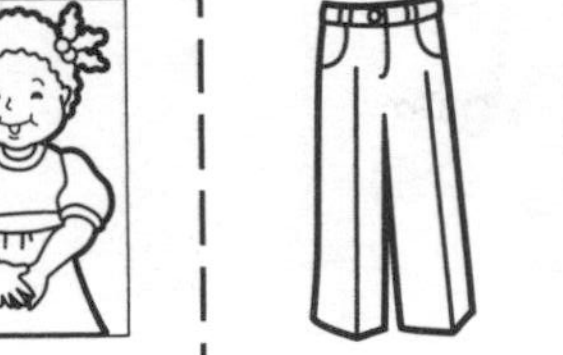

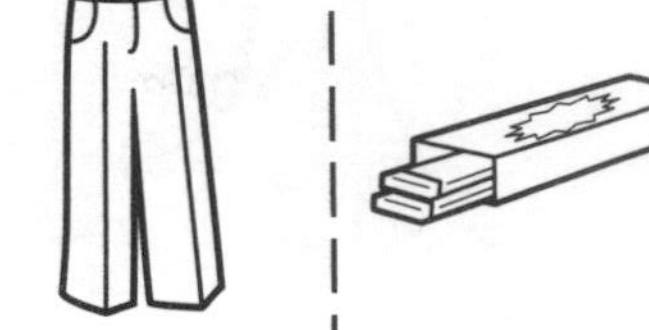

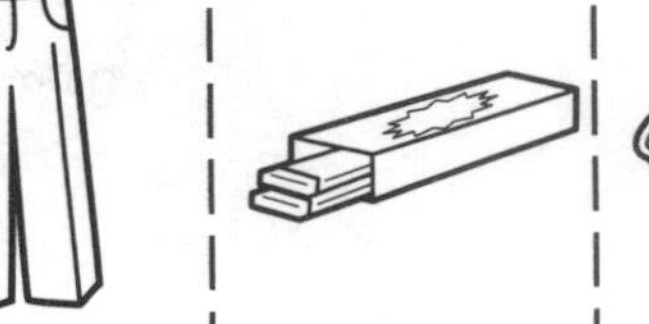

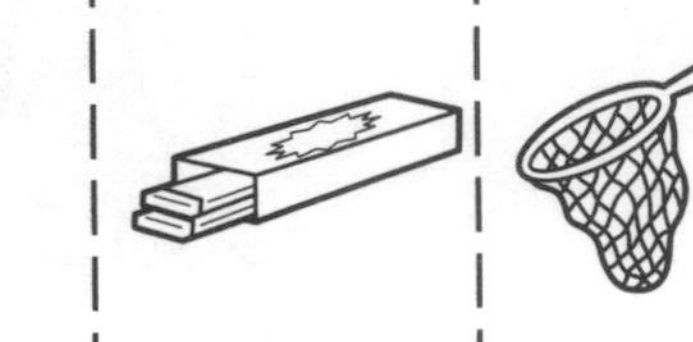

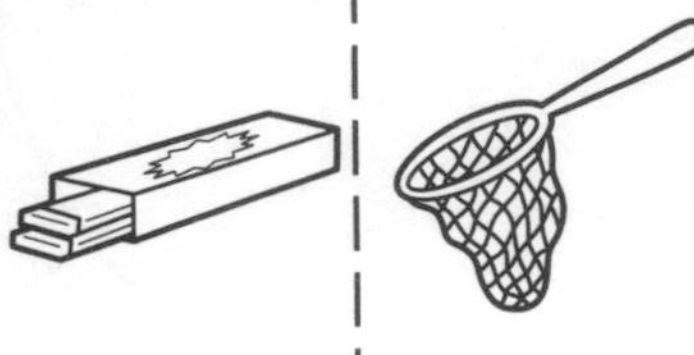

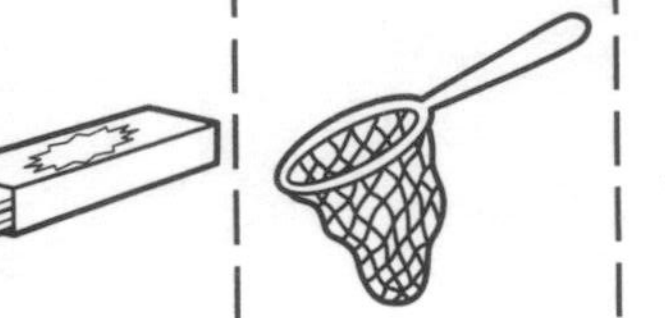

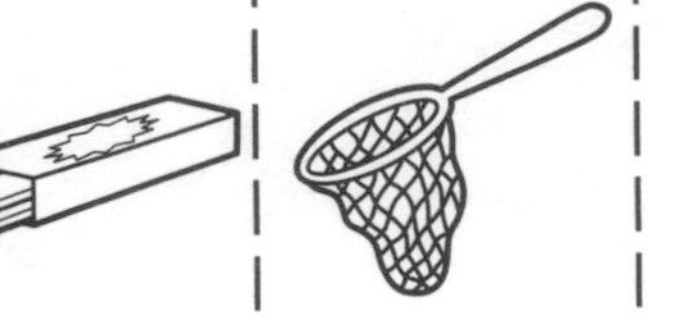

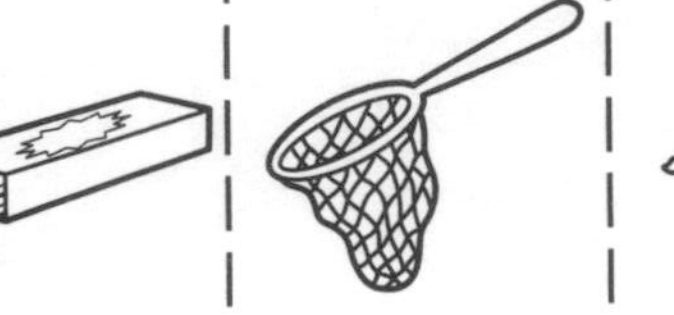

Name

Going for a Touchdown!

Color by the code.

Color Code

starts like —yellow

starts like —orange

starts like —green

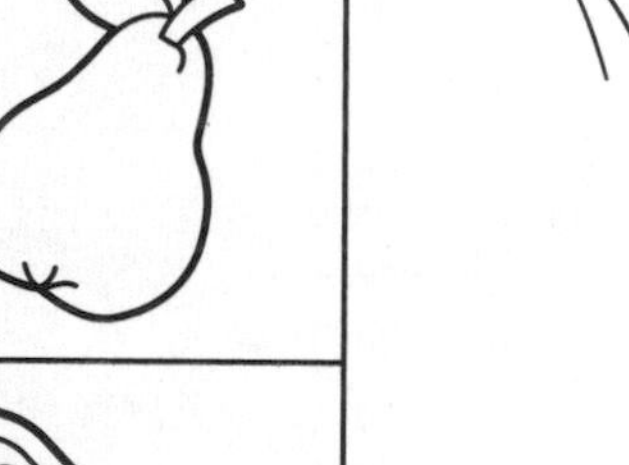

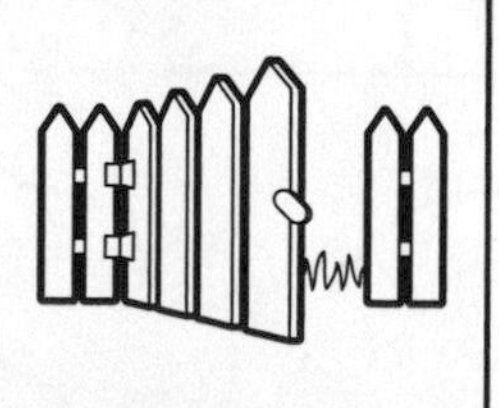

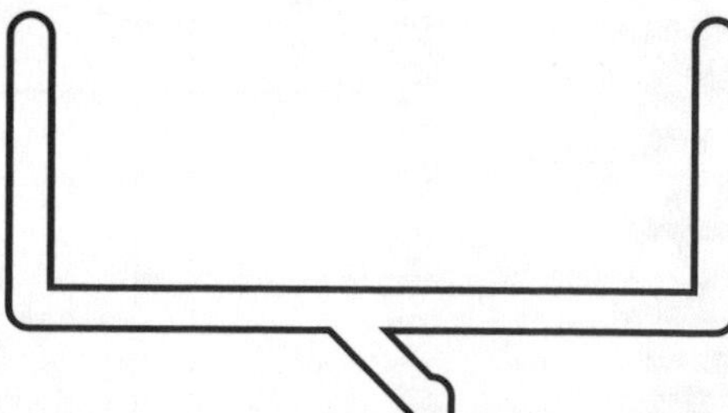

What color is Tiger's path?

Circle. yellow orange green

Name

Great Game!

Glue each set of pictures to a locker.

Note to the teacher: Have each child cut out a copy of a card set from page 24 before she begins the activity.

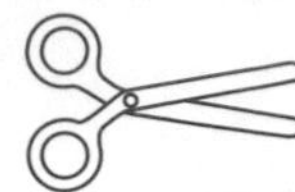

Cut. Sort by beginning sounds.

Beginning sounds: /g/, /n/, /p/ ▲▲▲

Cut. Sort by beginning sounds.

 Note to the teacher: Use with "Great Game!" on page 23.

Name

Laundry Day

Glue to match the beginning sounds.

Note to the teacher: Have each child cut out a copy of a card set from page 26 before she begins the activity.

Beginning sounds: /d/, /k/, /l/ ▲

Cut.

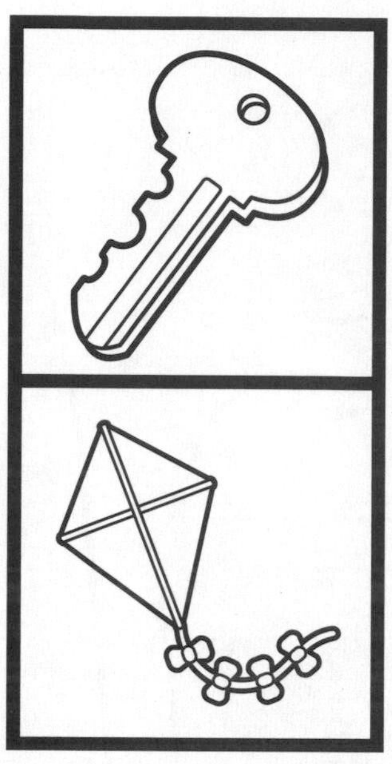

Beginning sounds: /d/, /k/, /l/ ▲

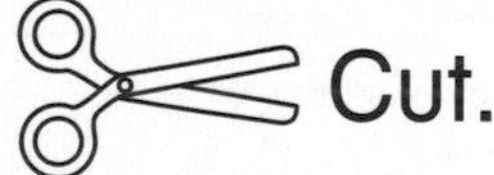

Cut.

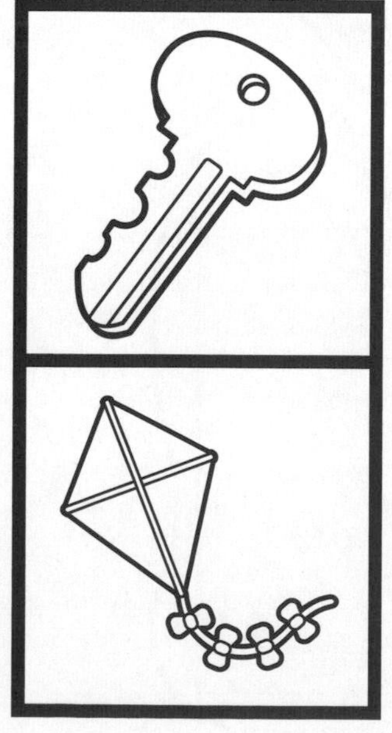

Note to the teacher: Use with "Laundry Day" on page 25.

Name

Time to Wash

Color the pictures that have the matching beginning sound.

Name

Laundry's Done!

Do all the pictures in each row have the same beginning sound?
Circle **Yes** or **No.**

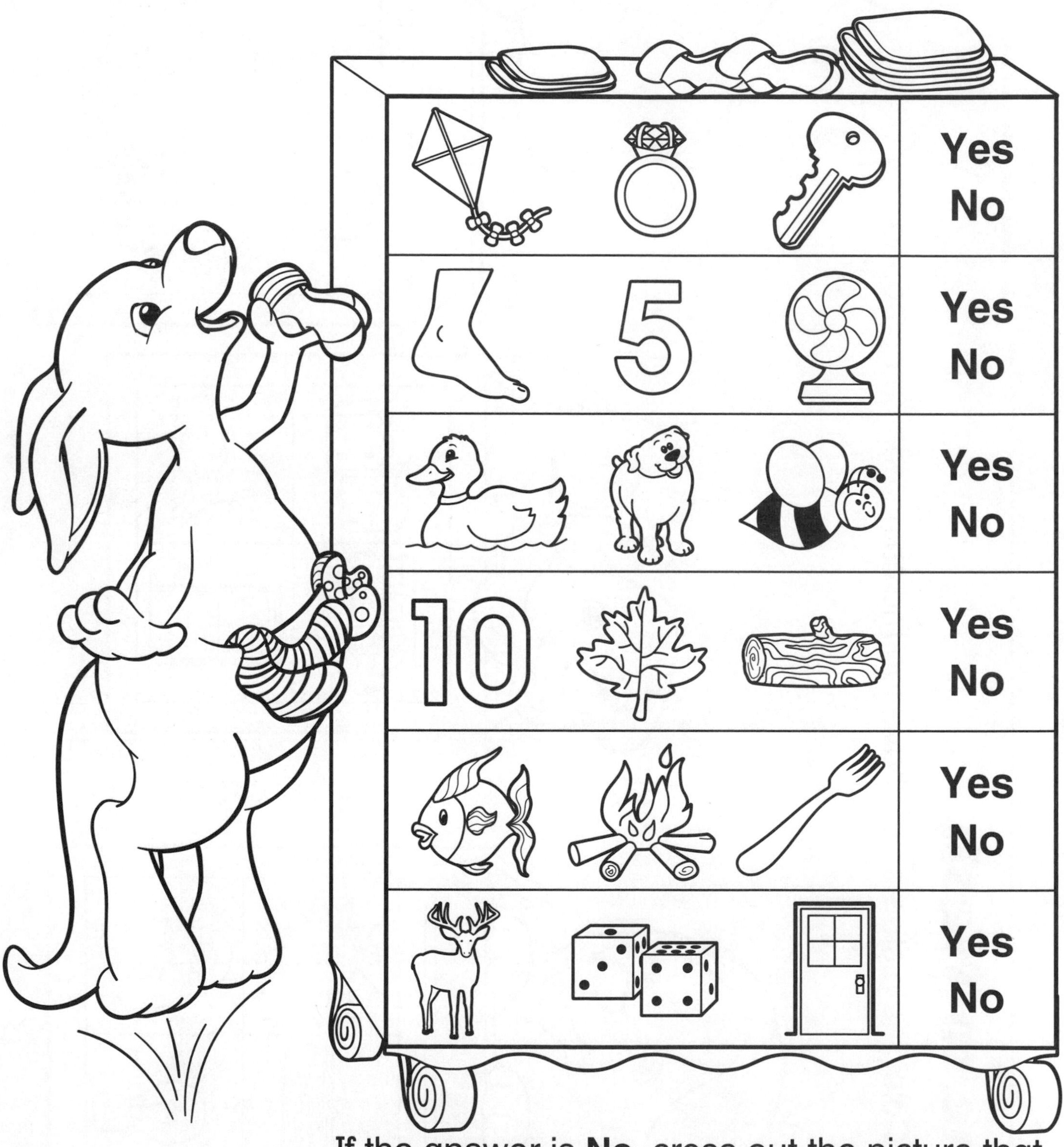

If the answer is **No**, cross out the picture that has a different beginning sound.

Name

High Flying

Glue to match the ending sounds.

Note to the teacher: Have each child cut out a copy of a card set from page 30 before he begins the activity.

Ending sounds: /l/, /n/, /t/ ▲

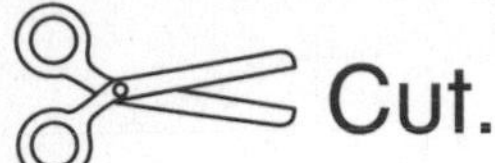
Cut.

Ending sounds: /l/, /n/, /t/ ▲

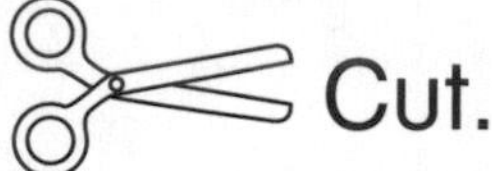
Cut.

 Note to the teacher: Use with "High Flying" on page 29.

Name

Skydiving

Color by the code.

Floating By

Color the pictures in each row that end with the same sound.

Cross out the picture that ends with a different sound.

Name

Fun at the Park

Glue to match.

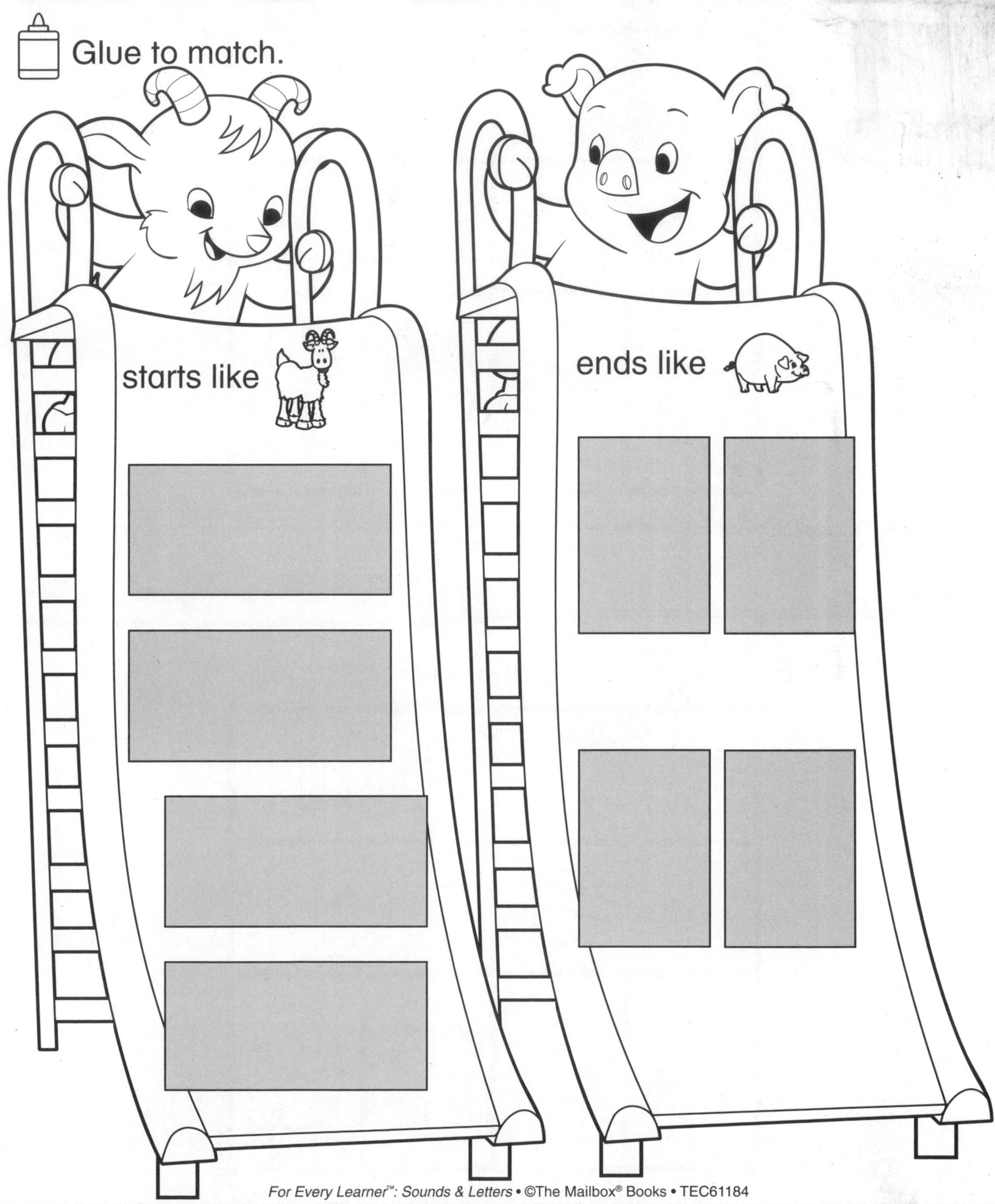

Note to the teacher: Have each child cut out a copy of a card set from page 34 before she begins the activity.

Cut. Sort by beginning and ending sound.

Beginning and ending sound: /g/

Cut. Sort by beginning and ending sound.

 Note to the teacher: Use with "Fun at the Park" on page 33.

Name

All Tangled Up!

Color by the code.

Color Code

starts like  —yellow

ends like  —red

Bicycle Buddies

Do the pictures in each row begin like [goat picture]?

Circle **Yes** or **No.**

			Yes No
GAS			Yes No
			Yes No

Cross out each picture that begins with a different sound.

Do the pictures in each row end like [pig picture]?

Circle **Yes** or **No.**

			Yes No
			Yes No
			Yes No

Cross out each picture that ends with a different sound.

Name

Picnic Time!

Name each picture.

Color the ◯ to show how many word parts.

 Name

Basket of Food

Color the ○ to show how many word parts.

Name

Sipping Picnic Punch

Glue to match the word parts.

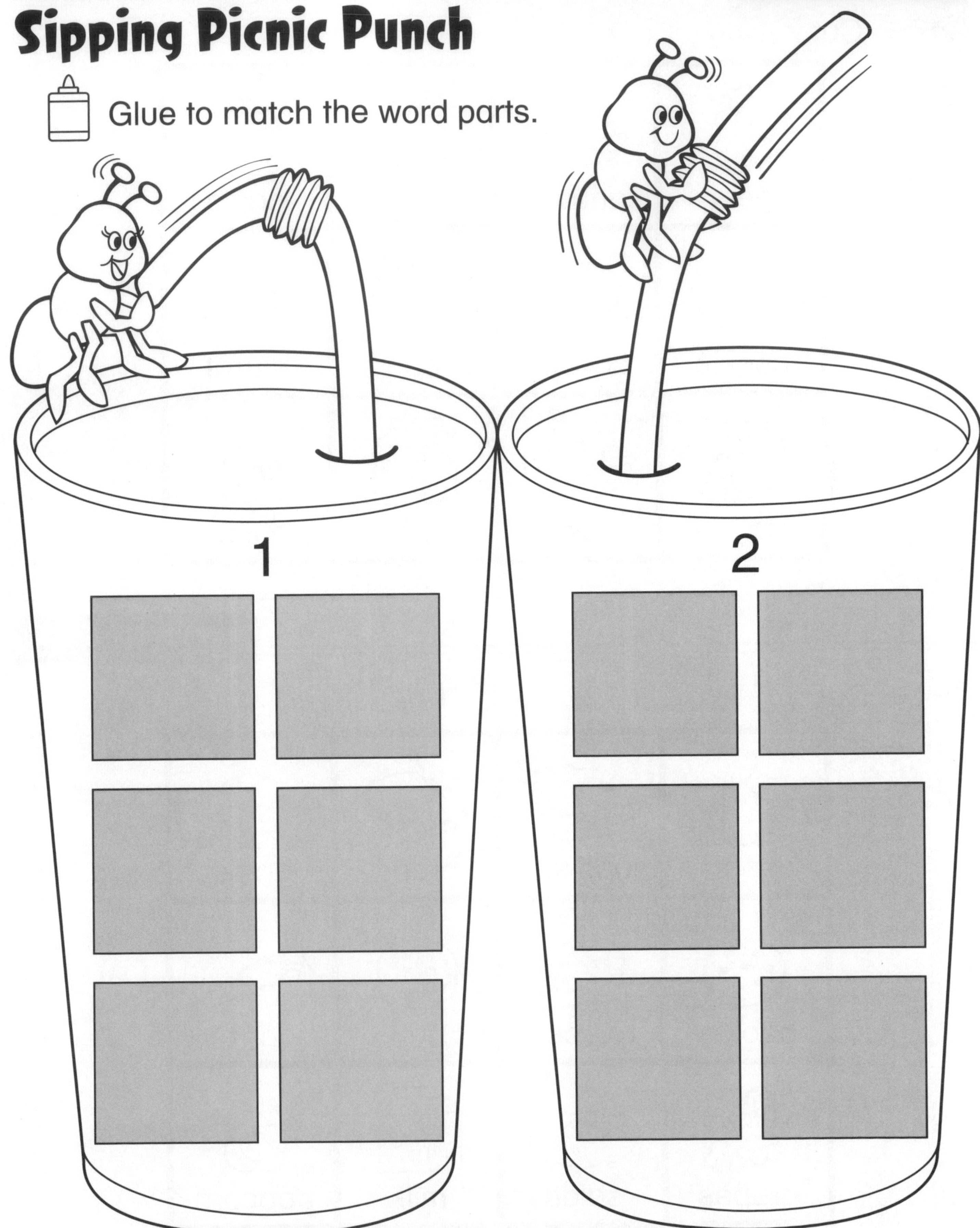

Note to the teacher: Have each child cut out a copy of a card set from page 40 before he begins the activity.

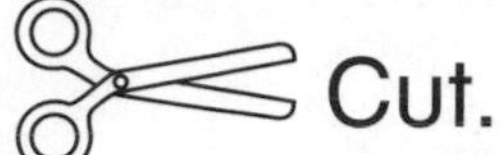

Cut.

Word parts ▲▲▲

Cut.

Note to the teacher: Use with “Sipping Picnic Punch” on page 39.

Name

Gopher Gets Glasses

Glue to make matching letter pairs.

Note to the teacher: Have each child cut out a copy of the cards from page 42 before she begins the activity.

 Cut.

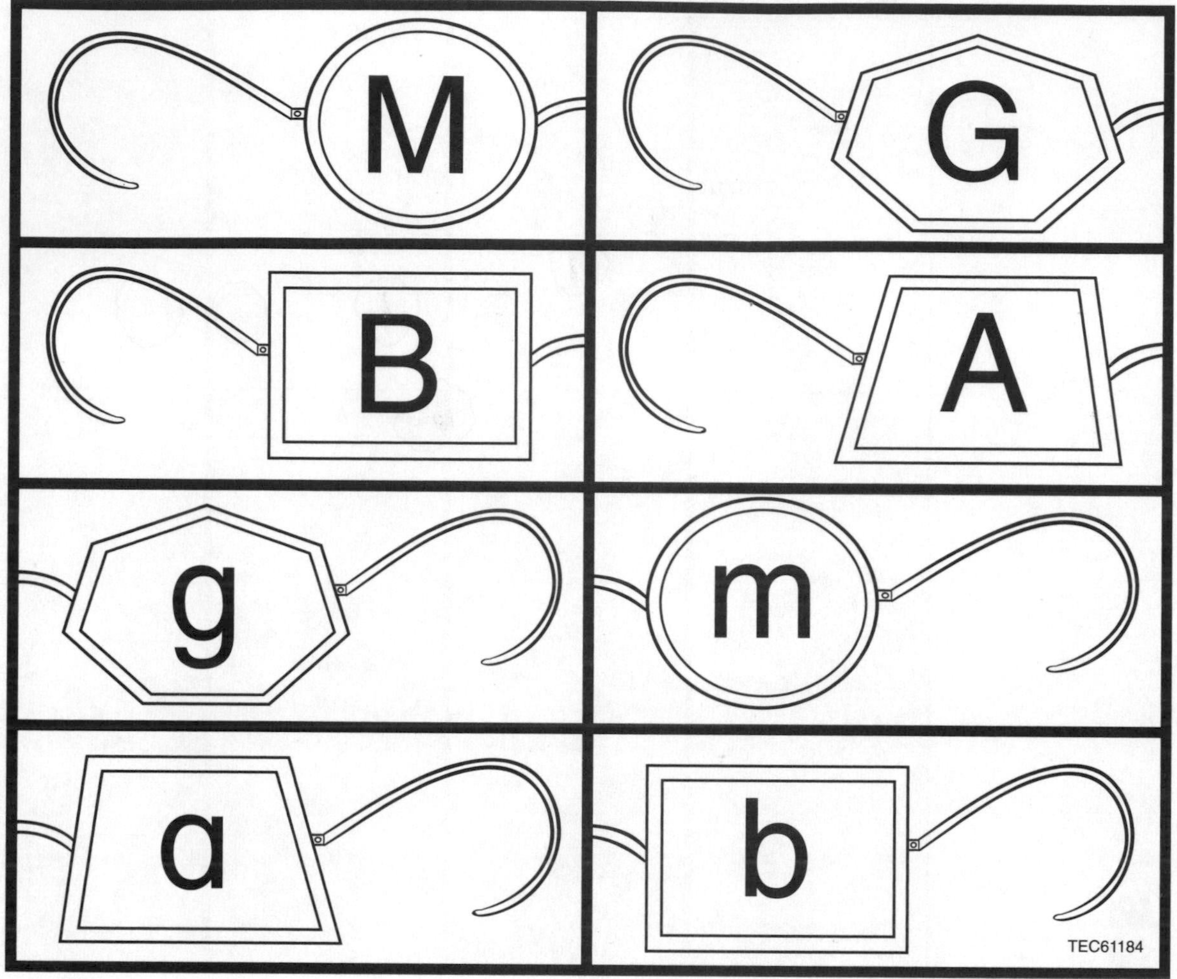

 Note to the teacher: Use with "Gopher Gets Glasses" on page 41.

Name

Gopher Needs His Glasses

Color the matching letter pairs.

	Ff	Cc	Ii
Qt	Rb	Ex	Kk
Gg	Dd	Mm	Ll
Oo	Ht	Je	Pa
Aa	Ss	Nn	

Gopher's Reading Glasses

Write to make matching letter pairs.

b ____			E ____
A ____	K ____	I ____	j ____
G ____	V ____	c ____	D ____
m ____	T ____	L ____	o ____
S ____	n ____	Q ____	u ____
f ____	R ____	P ____	W ____
H ____	y ____	X ____	z ____

Name

Sneaky Squirrels

Glue to match each picture with its beginning letter.

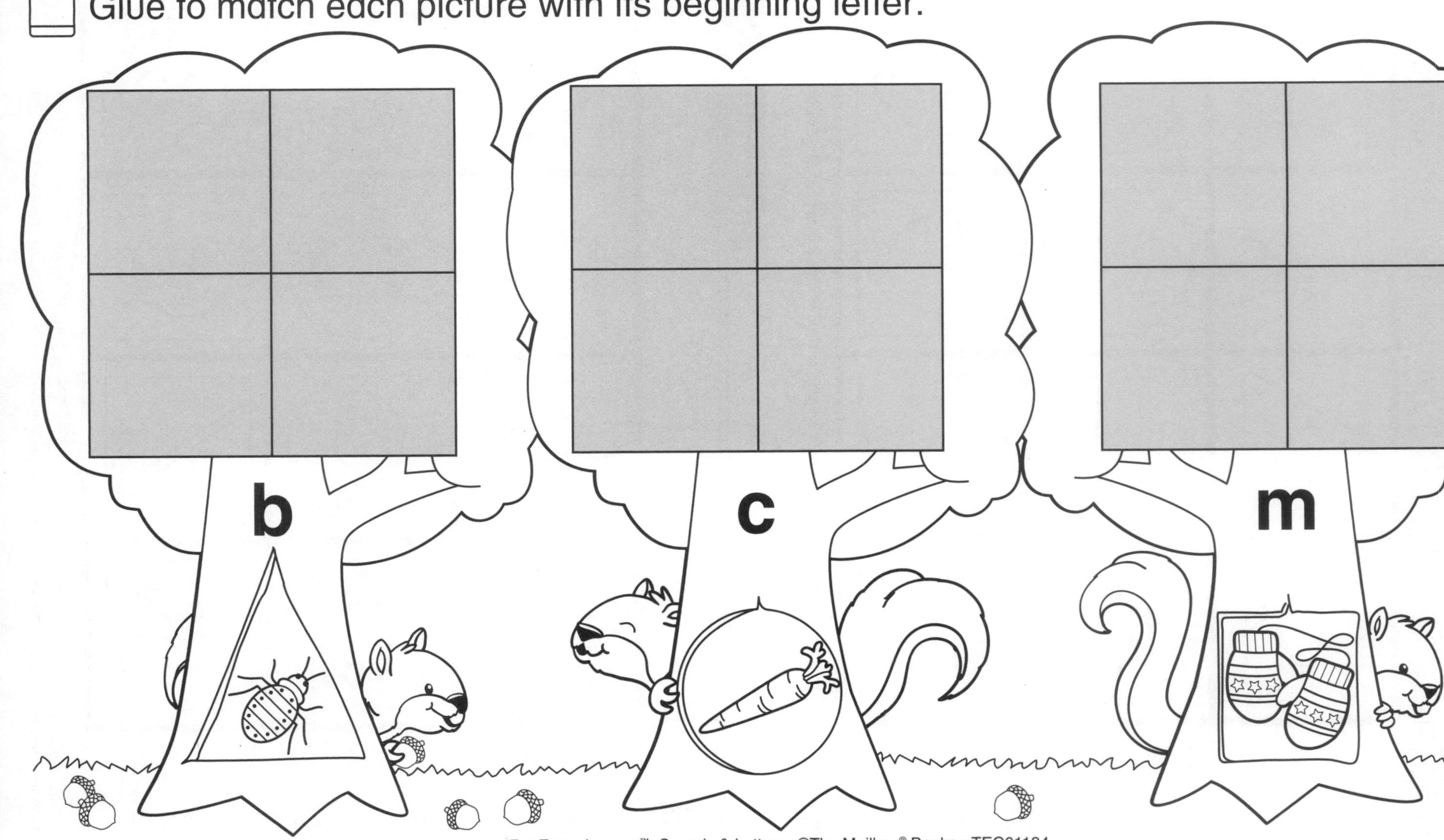

Note to the teacher: Have each child cut out a copy of a card set from page 46 before she begins the activity.

Initial consonants: *b, c, m* ▲

Cut.

Initial consonants: *b, c, m* ▲

Cut.

 Note to the teacher: Use with "Sneaky Squirrels" on page 45.

Name

Collecting Treasures

Color by the code.

Name

It's Dinnertime

Write **b, c,** or **m** to make each word.

Name

Bubble Bath

Color by the code.

Name

What to Wear?

Glue to match each picture with its beginning letter.

g

h

t

 Note to the teacher: Have each child cut out a copy of a card set from page 51 before he begins the activity.

Cut.

Initial consonants: *g, h, t* ▲▲

Cut.

Note to the teacher: Use with "What to Wear?" on page 50.

Name

Looking Good

Cross out the picture whose beginning letter does not match.

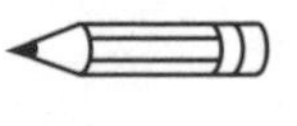

Write the beginning letter of the other pictures.

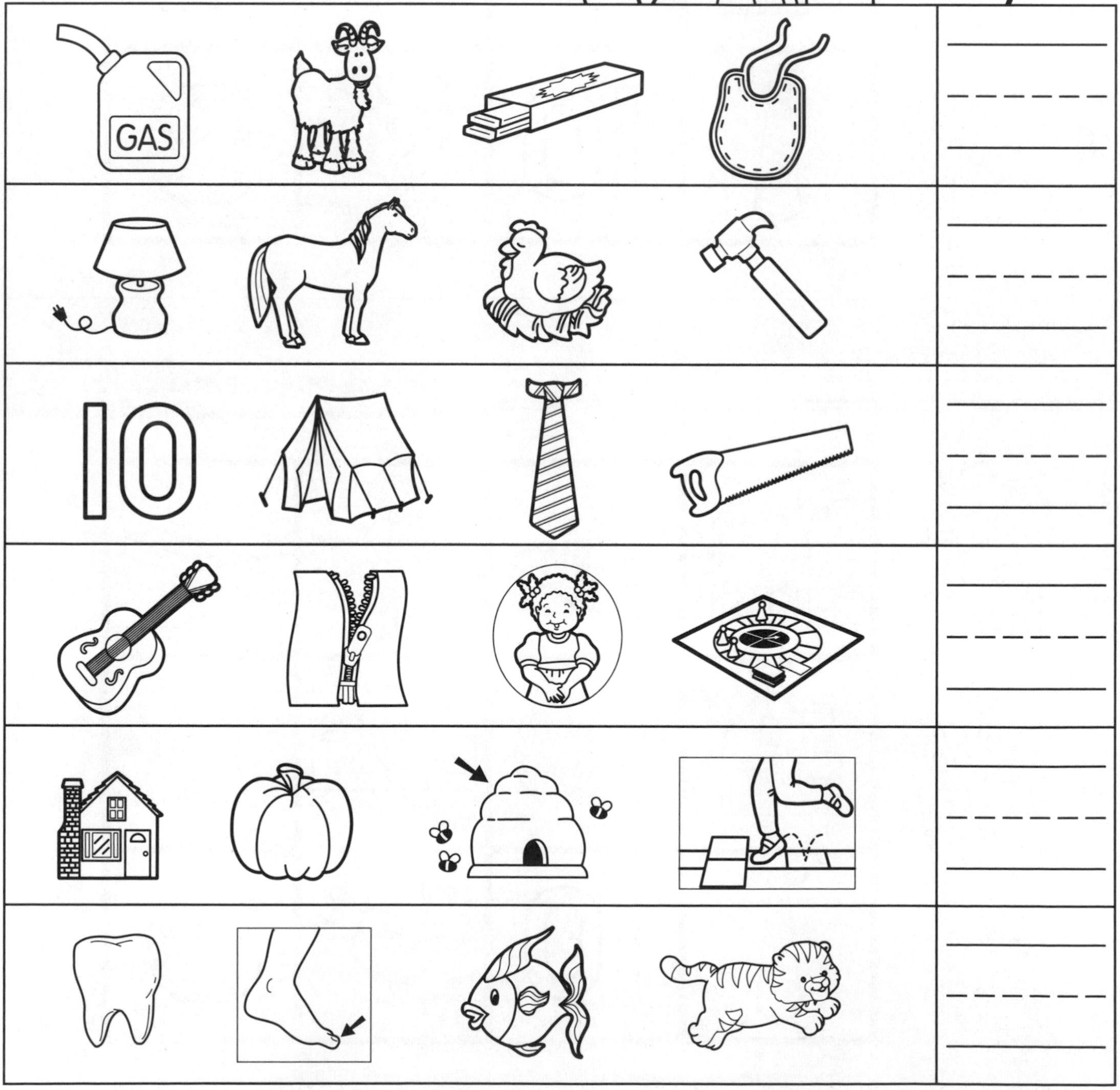

GAS				

Name

Lily Pad Lounging

Cut.
Glue to match each picture with its beginning letter.

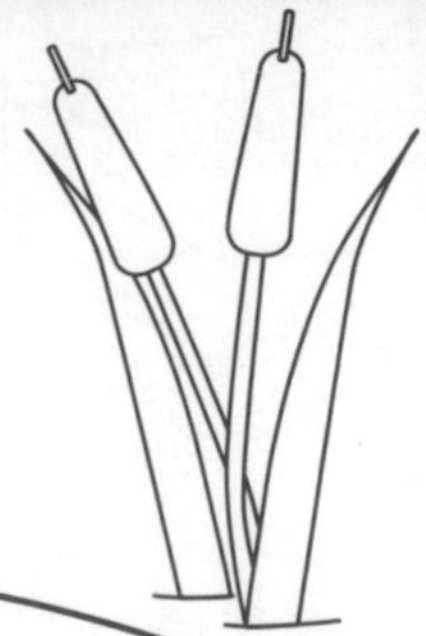

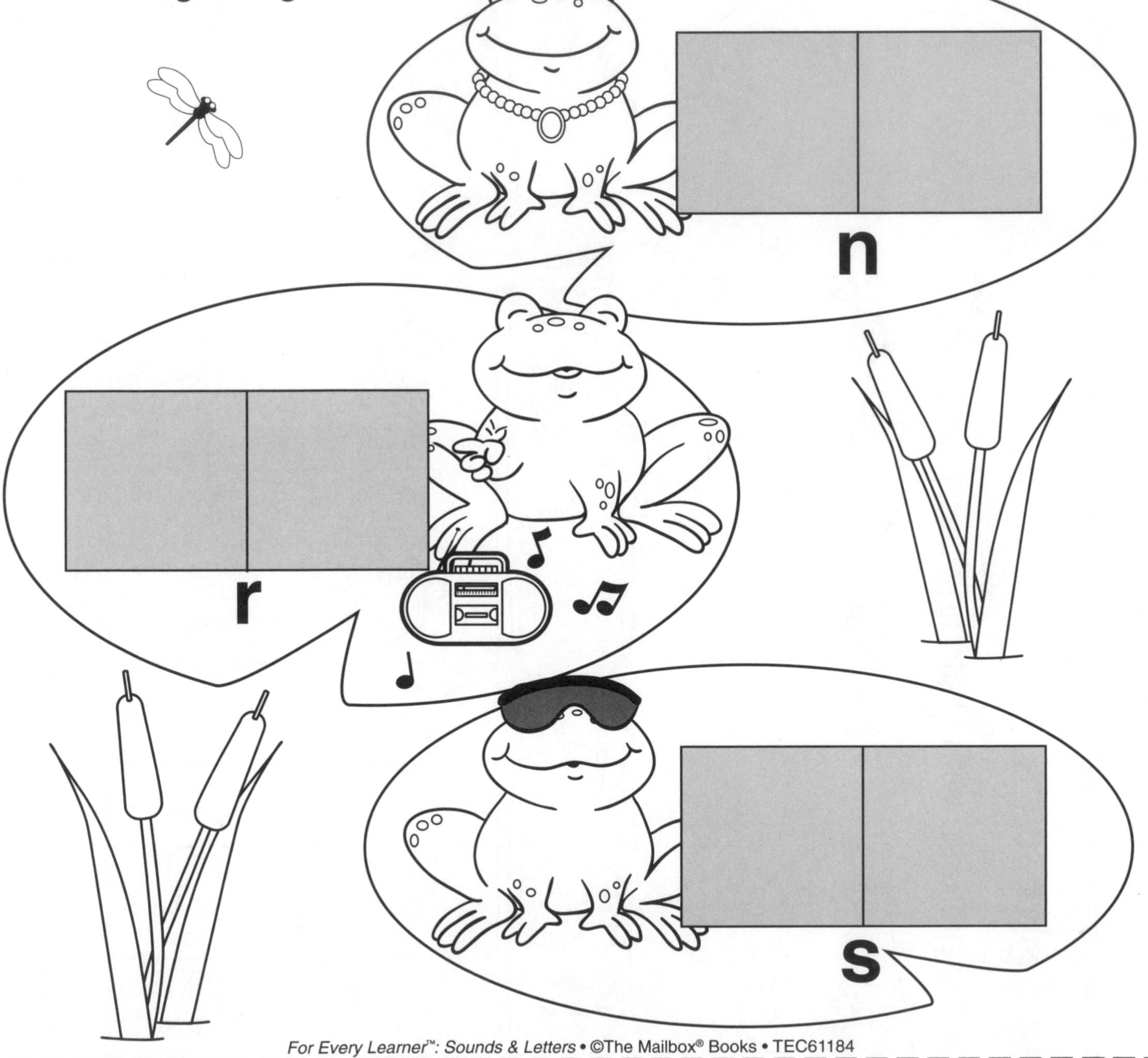

n

r

s

Frogs on Logs

Color the pictures with matching beginning letters.

Name

Pond Play

Glue each set of cards on a lily pad.

Write the beginning letter.

Note to the teacher: Have each student complete a copy of a card set from page 56 before she begins the activity.

Write **n, r,** or **s** to make each word.
Cut.
Sort by the beginning letter.

___ at	___ oap	___ ut	___ ug
___ ock	___ est	___ adio	___ aw
___ ine	___ ake	___ eal	___ et

Initial consonants: *n, r, s* ▲▲▲

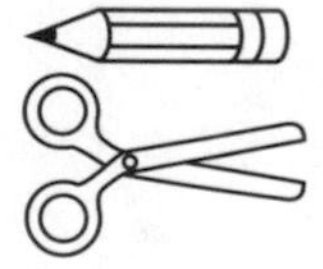

Write **n, r,** or **s** to make each word.
Cut.
Sort by the beginning letter.

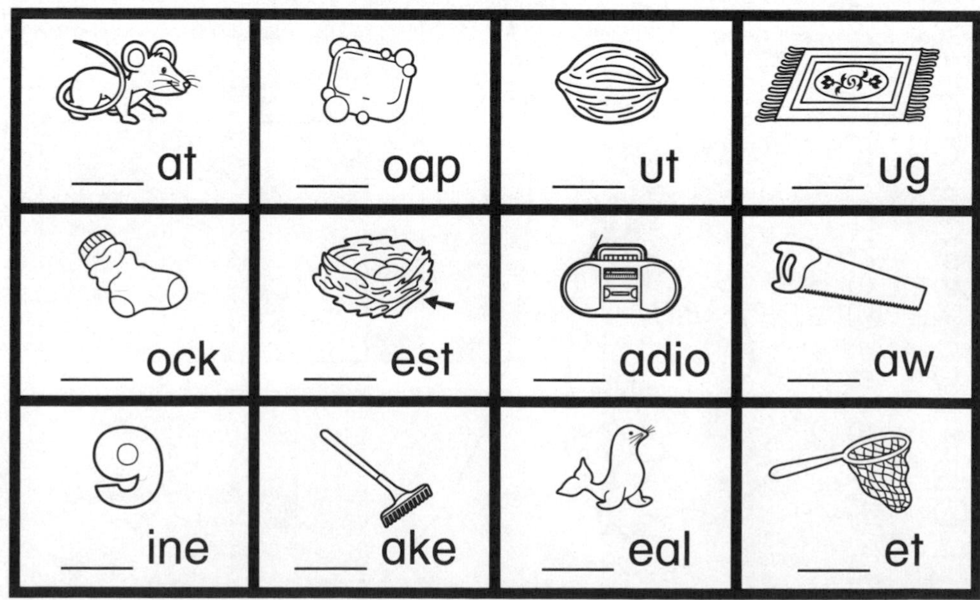

___ at	___ oap	___ ut	___ ug
___ ock	___ est	___ adio	___ aw
___ ine	___ ake	___ eal	___ et

 Note to the teacher: Use with "Pond Play" on page 55.

Name

Jazzy Jugglers

Glue to match each picture with its beginning or ending letter.

STOP

p-

-p

p-

-p

Note to the teacher: Have each student cut out a copy of a card set from page 58 before he begins the activity.

Cut.

Initial and final consonants: p ▲

Cut.

 Note to the teacher: Use with “Jazzy Jugglers” on page 57.

Name

Balancing Act

Color the pictures that begin with **p.**

Color the pictures that end with **p.**

Name

Clowning Around

Circle yes or no.

Do both pictures
begin with p?

	yes no
	yes no
	yes no
	yes no

Do both pictures
end with p?

	yes no
	yes no
	yes no
	yes no

Name

On the Road

Glue to match the word families.

Note to the teacher: Have each child cut out a copy of a card set from page 62 before he begins the activity.

Cut.

Word families: -an, -at

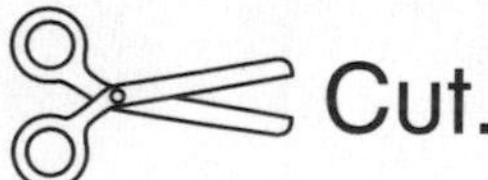
Cut.

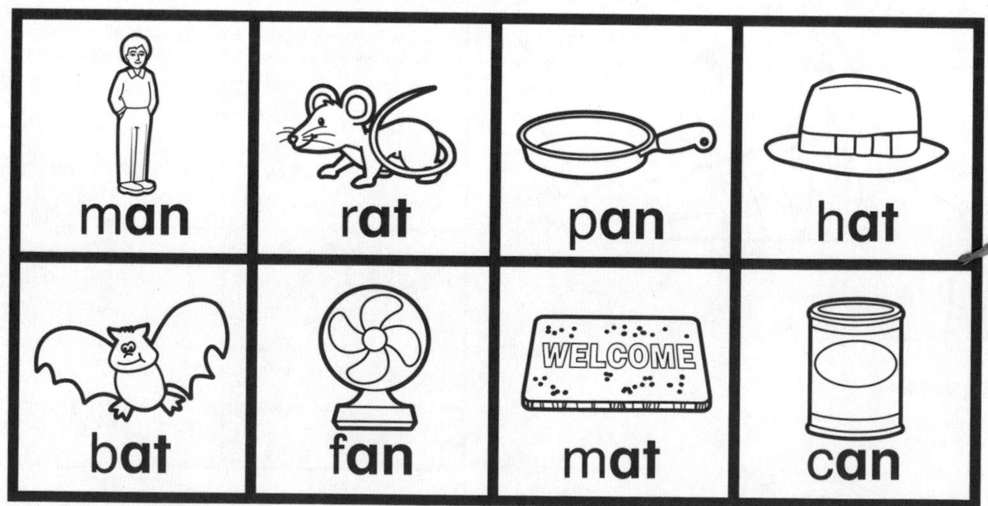

 Note to the teacher: Use with "On the Road" on page 61.

Name

Lots to Label

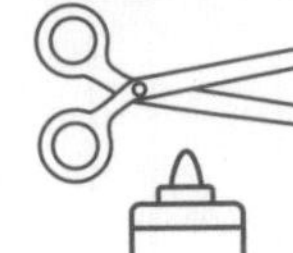

Cut.

Glue to match each word to a picture.

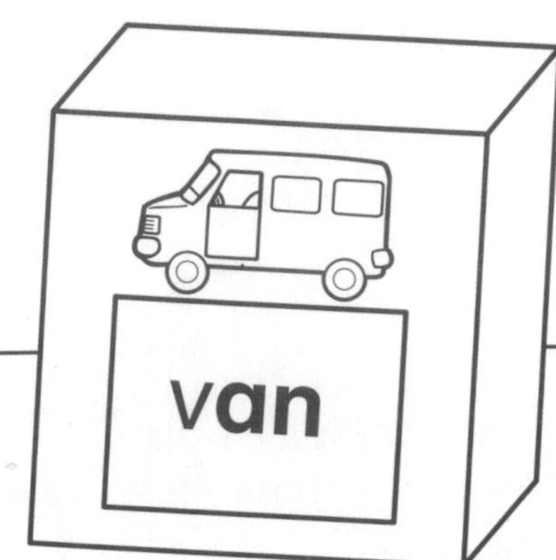

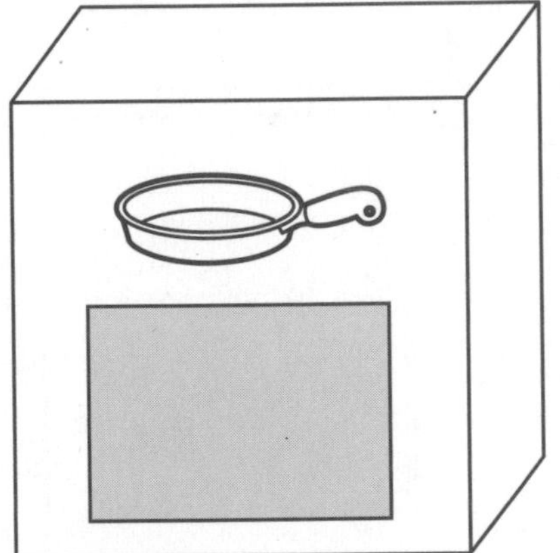

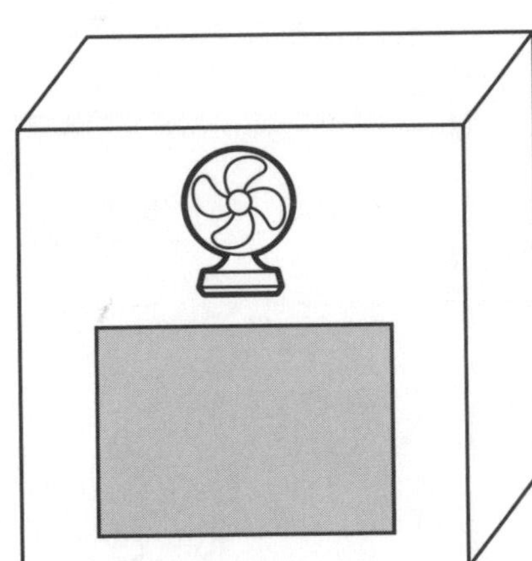

bat	pan	fan	hat	man	rat

Stacking Boxes

Write **-an** or **-at** to finish each word.

Color the pictures by the code.

Color Code

-an as in p**an** — yellow

-at as in c**at** — red

r______

c______

v______

m______

b______

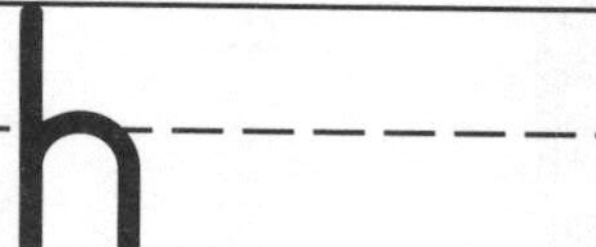

m______

h______

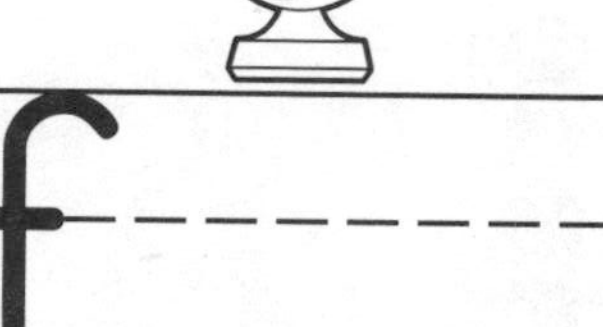

f______

Name

Going Surfing

Cut.

Glue to match the word families.

-ig

-in

wig

fin

big

pin

dig

win

Name

Catch Some Rays

Glue each picture to match its word family.

Glue each word below its matching picture.

pig

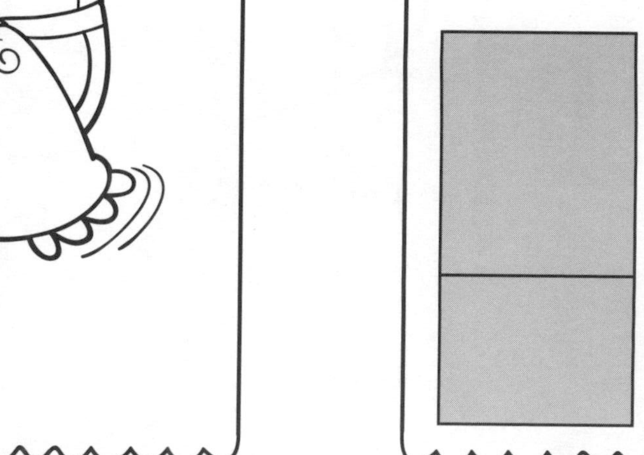

fin

Note to the teacher: Have each child cut out a copy of a card set from page 67 before she begins the activity.

Word families: *-ig, -in* ▲▲

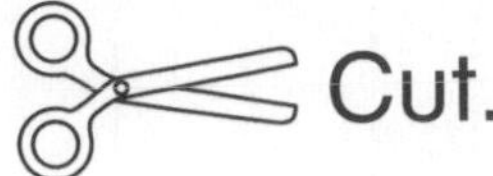 Cut.

dig	pin
win	big
wig	twin

Word families: *-ig, -in* ▲▲

 Cut.

dig	pin
win	big
wig	twin

Note to the teacher: Use with "Catch Some Rays" on page 66.

Name

Riding the Waves

Write a word to match each picture.

Name

To the Store

Color the pictures that end with **op** as in STOP.

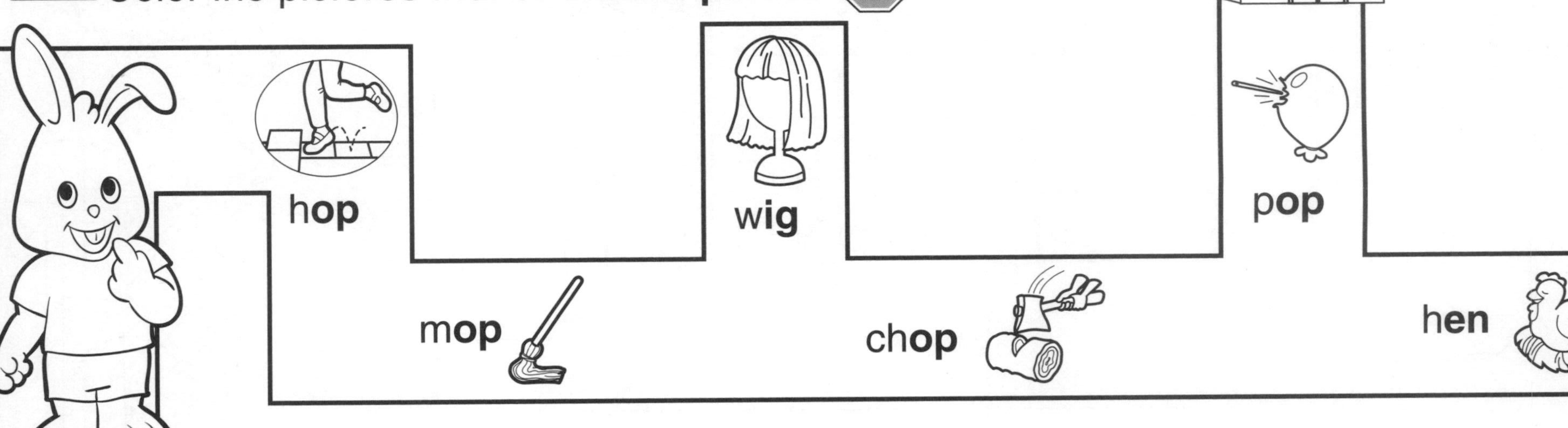

Color the pictures that end with **ot** as in [knot picture].

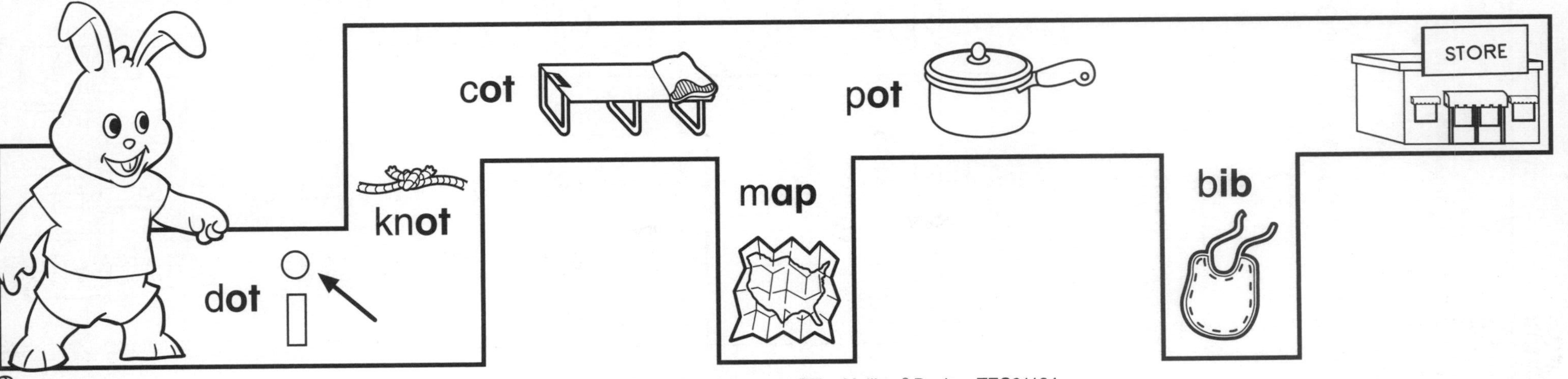

Name

Busy Shopper

Color by the code.

Color Code

-op as in st**op**  —purple

-ot as in p**ot**  —orange

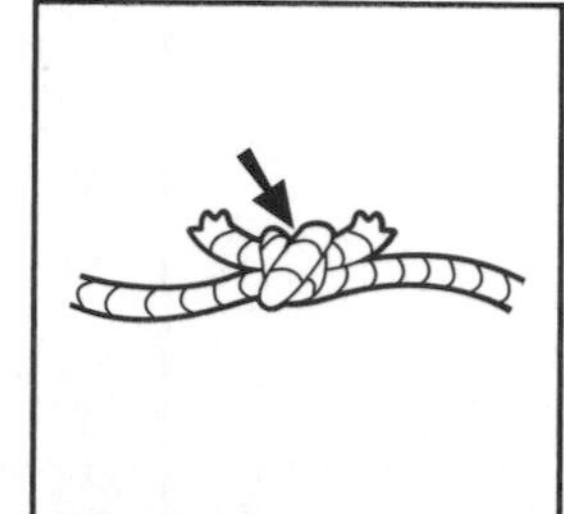
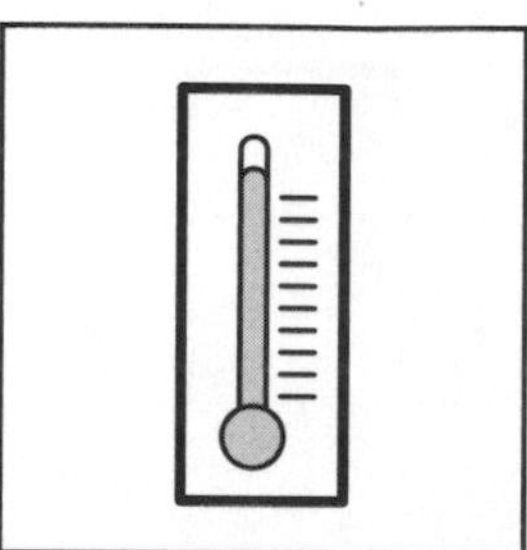

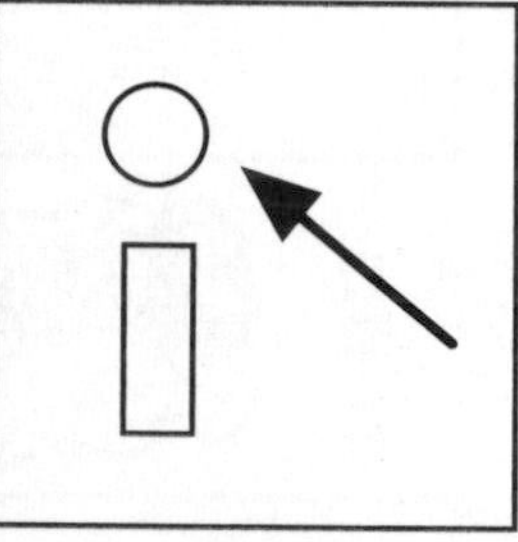

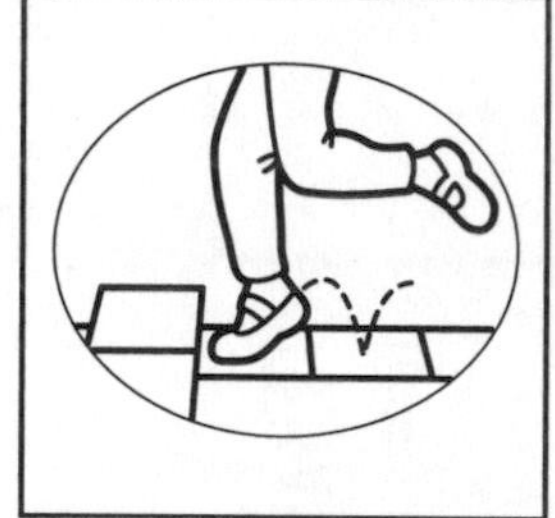
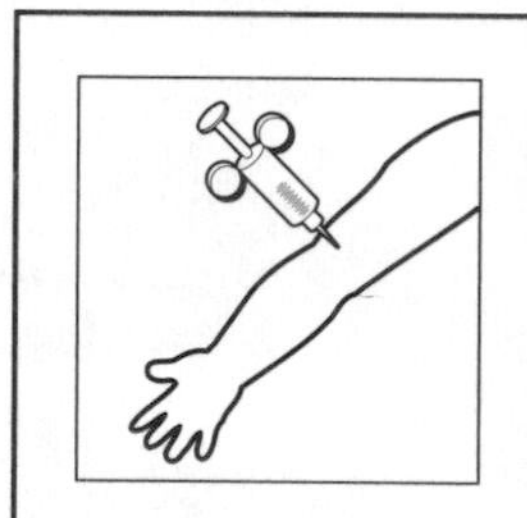
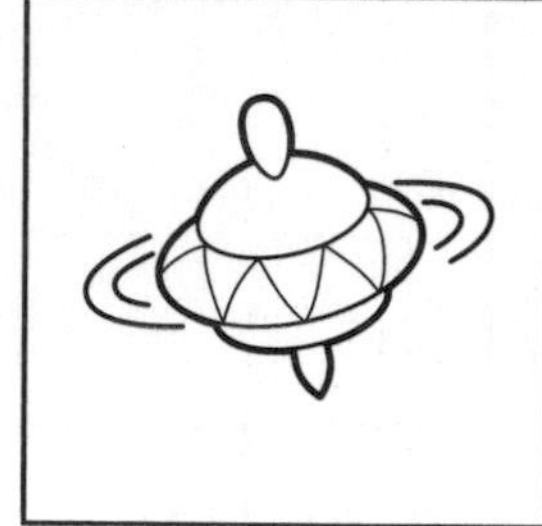

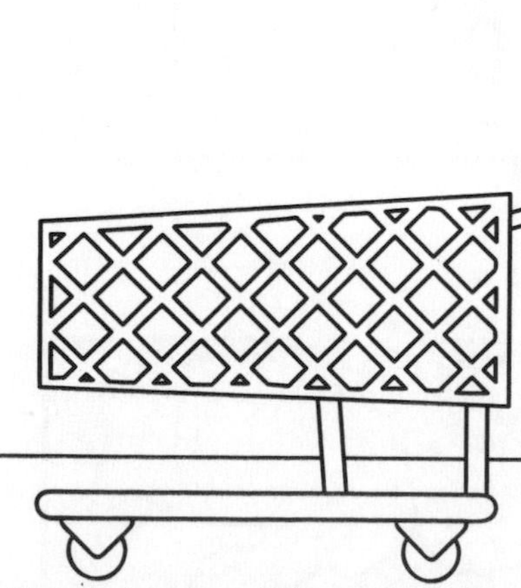

Name

Watch Out!

Glue each card set in the correct cart.

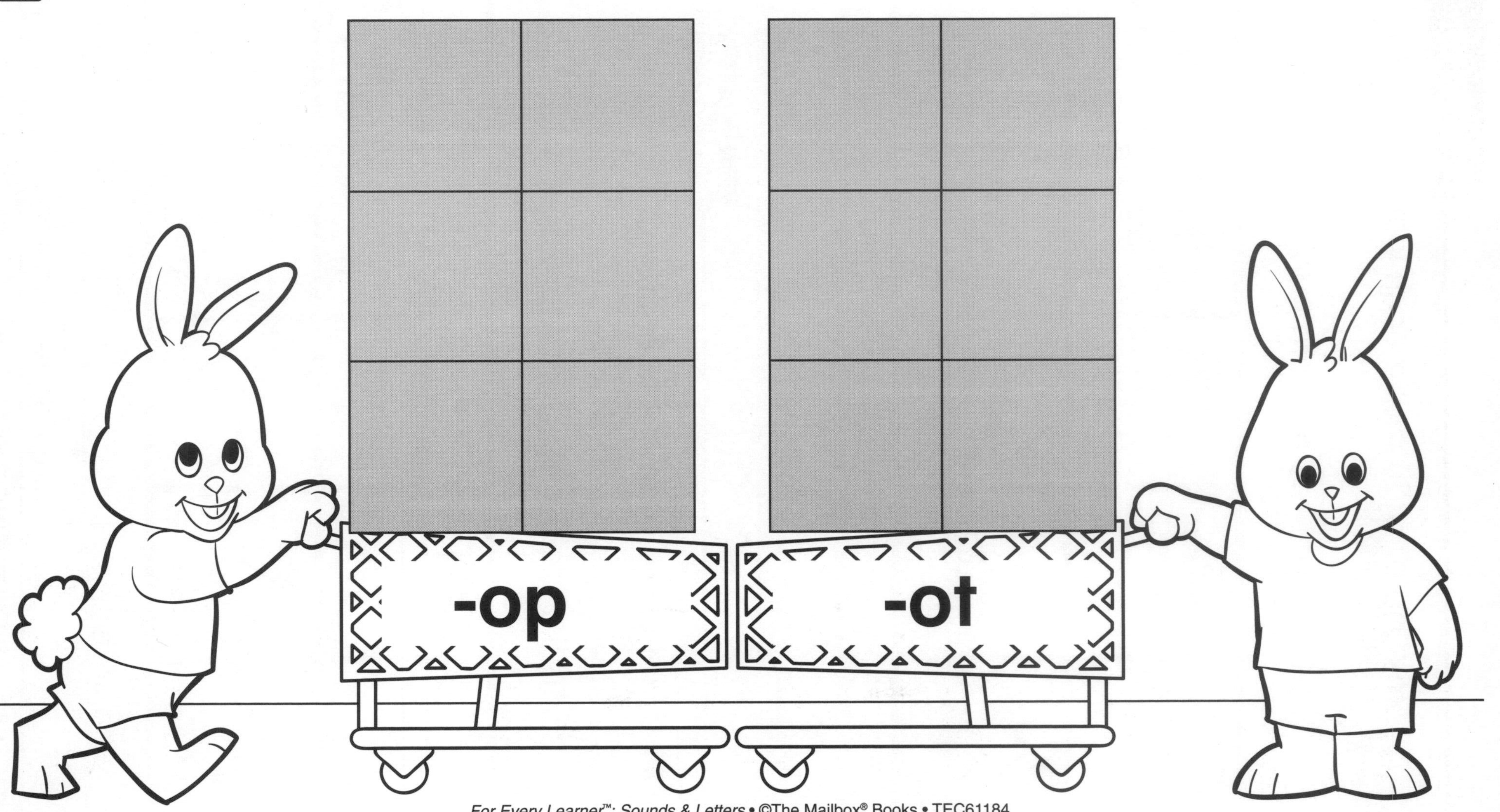

Note to the teacher: Have each student complete a card set from page 72 before he begins this activity.

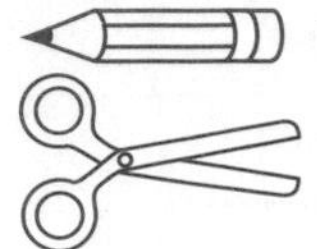

Write **op** or **ot** to make each word.
Cut.
Sort the pictures by word family.

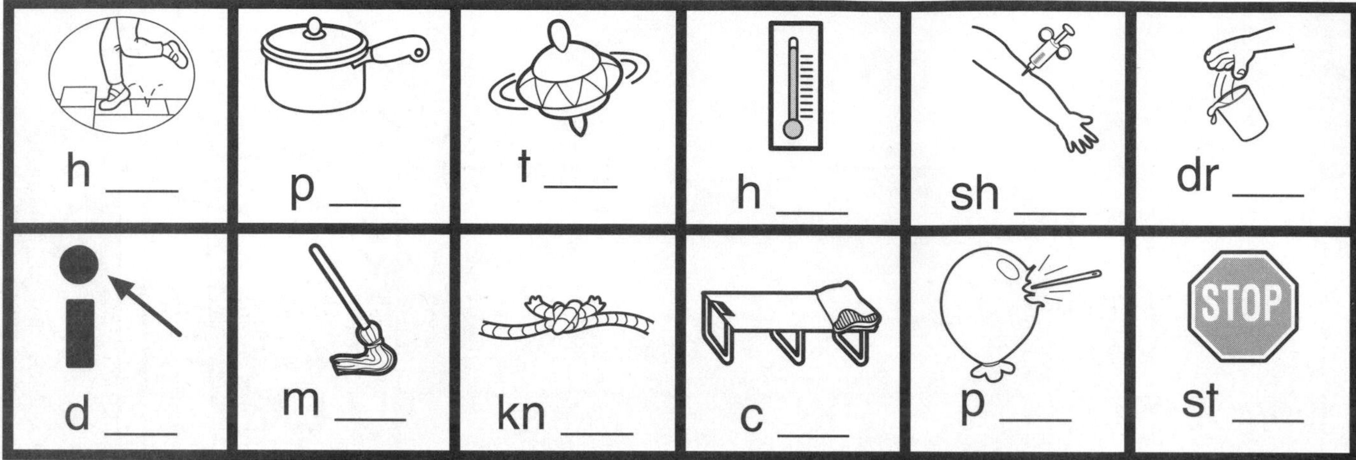

Word families: *-op, -ot*

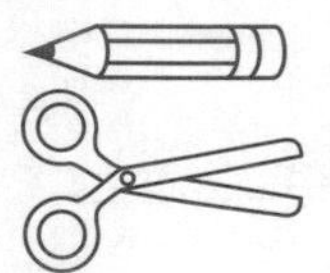

Write **op** or **ot** to make each word.
Cut.
Sort the pictures by word family.

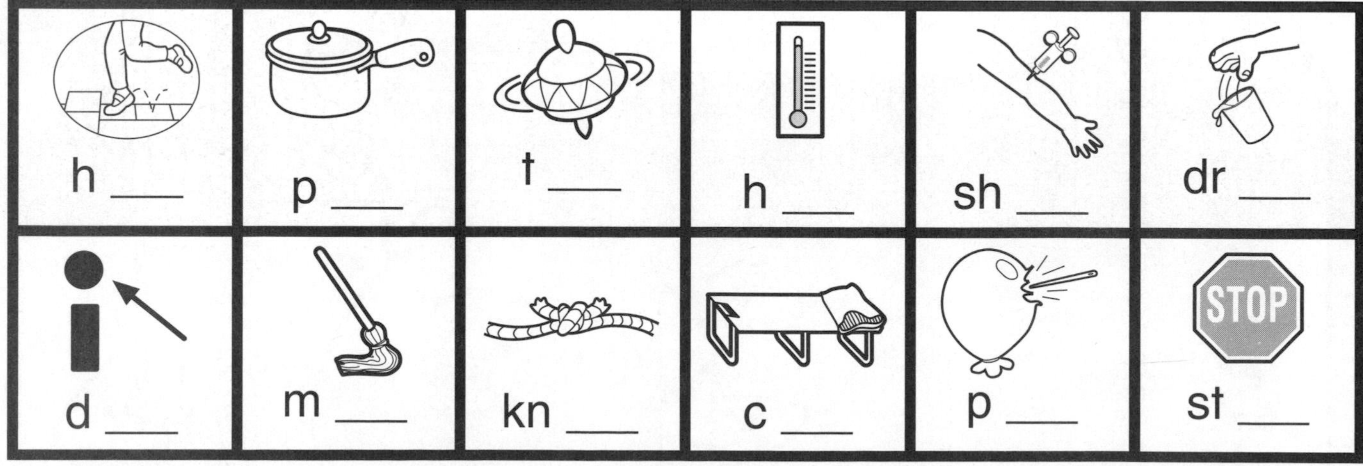

 Note to the teacher: Use with "Watch Out!" on page 71.

Name

Ice Cream Sandwich Treats

Glue to match the vowel sounds.

Note to the teacher: Have each child cut out a copy of a card set from page 74 before he begins the activity.

Cut.

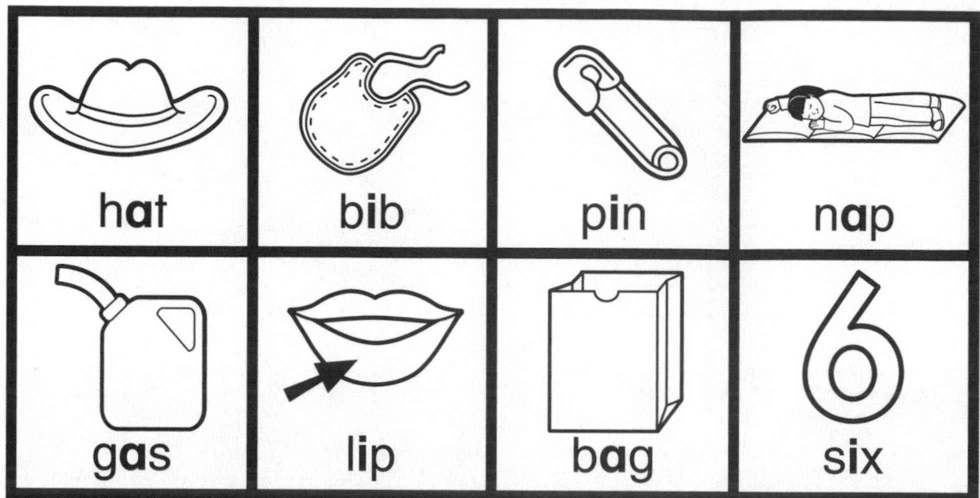

Short vowels: *a, i* ▲

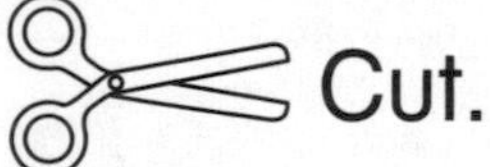
Cut.

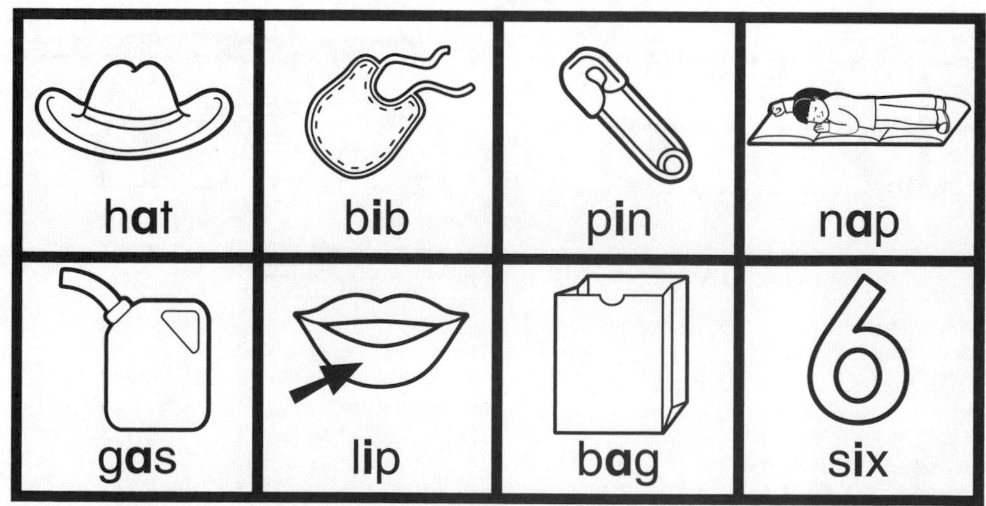

Note to the teacher: Use with "Ice Cream Sandwich Treats" on page 73.

Name

Super Sundae!

Color by the code.

Write the missing vowel.

Name

Yummy Shakes

Cross out each picture that does not have the short **a** sound.

Cross out each picture that does not have the short **i** sound.

Write each word. Use the word bank.

 short **a**

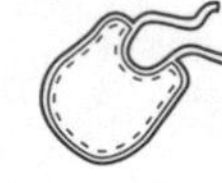 short **i**

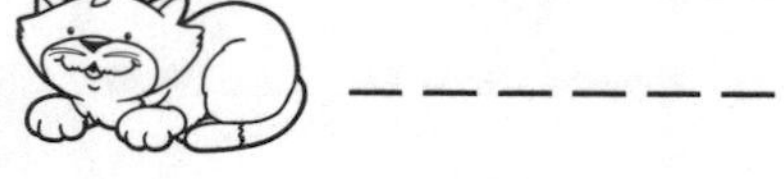

Word Bank

bag six wig cat pig nap

Name

To the Hive!

Glue to match the vowel sounds.

Note to the teacher: Have each child cut out a copy of the card set on page 78 before he begins the activity.

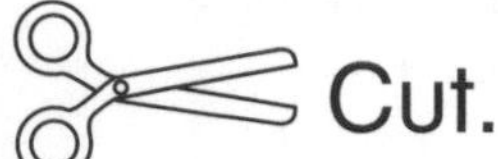
Cut.

Short vowels: *e, o, u* ▲

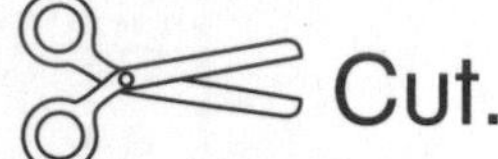
Cut.

Short vowels: *e, o, u* ▲

Cut.

 Note to the teacher: Use with "To the Hive!" on page 77.

Name

What's the Buzz?

Write each missing vowel.

Color a bee for each matching vowel.

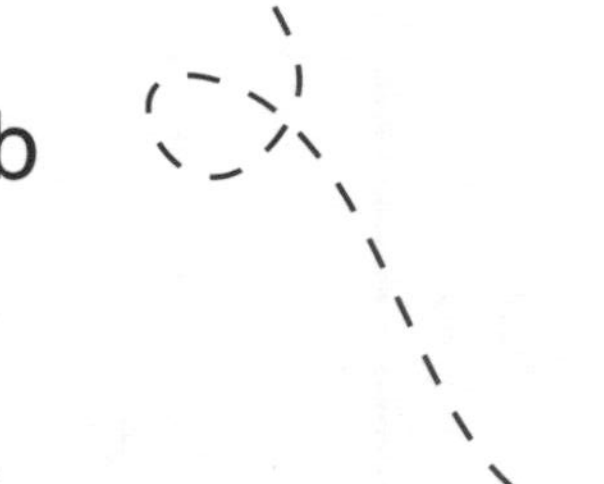
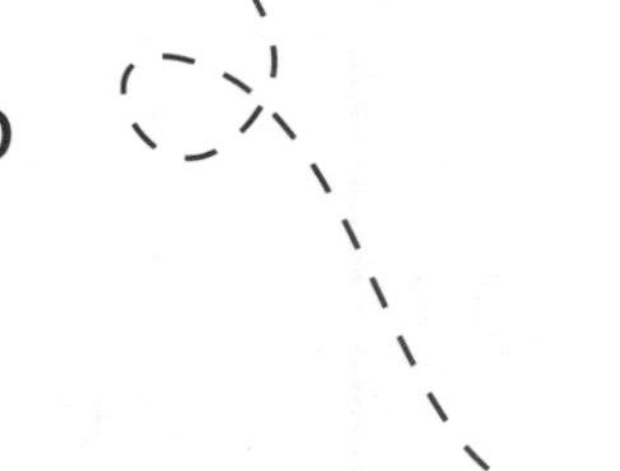

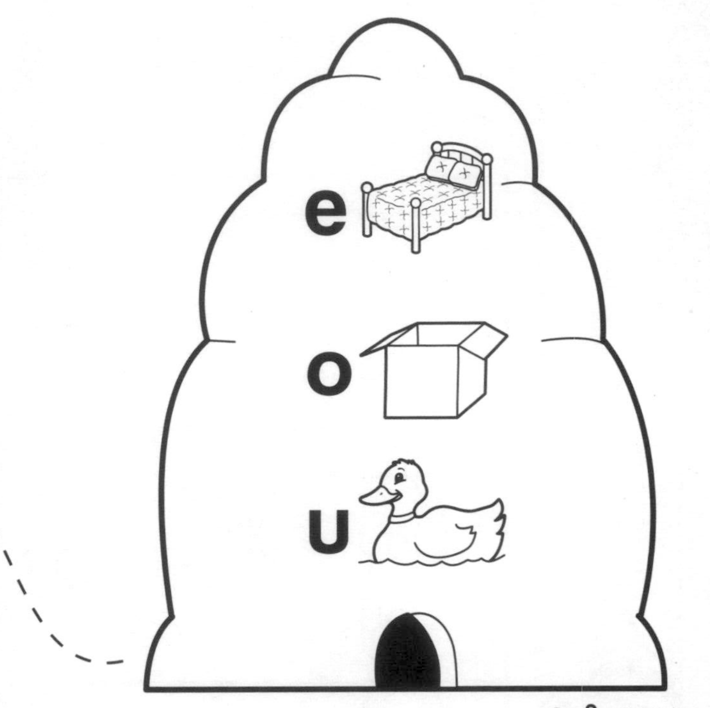
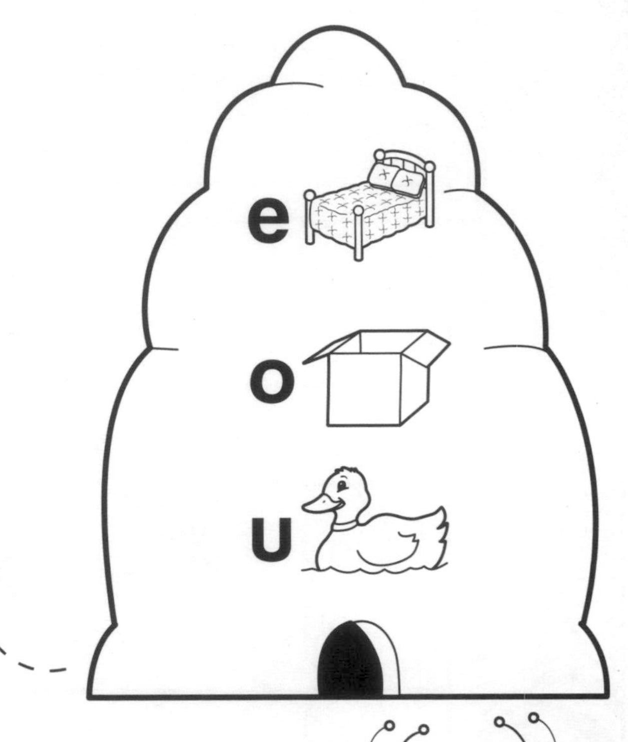

1. b ___ g

2.  w ___ b

3. m ___ p

4.  n ___ t

5. f ___ x

6.  l ___ g

7.  n ___ t

8.  p ___ t

Flowers for Bees

Circle the correct word.

Color the matching flower.

 leg log lug	 bed bid bad	 pet pot pit
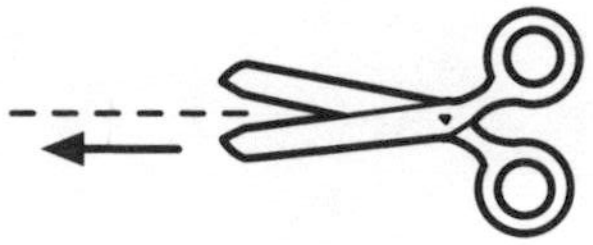 cat cut cot	 net not nut	 net not nut
 tin ten tan	 bug big beg	 cat cut cot